Watch My

by

Geoff Saunders

First performed as a rehearsed reading at the Goodrich Theatre, Putney, on 26th May 1996, with the following cast:

Jeff . . . . *Adrian Blake*

Mark . . . . *Ian Higham*

Directed by Geoff Saunders

Sound by CJ Lampard

Lighting by Caroline Ferris

Characters

Jeff

Mark

Two spaces with indefinite borders. To one side is an electric fan with a small stool directly in front of it; an unbound typed manuscript stands on the stool. This is MARK's space. To the other side is a typewriter or computer: this is JEFF's space.

When the play begins, MARK's space is lit. MARK and JEFF are both standing. MARK is holding a CD player's remote control.

JEFF: Look, we really need to talk.

MARK: *(to the audience)* Makes your blood run cold, doesn't it? You've all been through this. You're in a relationship, everything's great fun, you're fond of each other, then one of you says...

JEFF: *(exactly as before)* Look, we really need to talk.

MARK: *(to the audience)* Suddenly it's not just fun any more. Suddenly it's - capital S - Serious. And there's no going back. In my experience, the conversation that begins...

JEFF: *(exactly as before)* Look, we need to talk.

MARK: *(to the audience)* - quite often leads to the end of the relationship. The last guy I went out with - before Jeff *(He indicates JEFF.)* - suddenly decided we "needed to talk." It was only about some tiny incompatibility which, dealt with on its own, could have been sorted out really easily, but, oh, no, no-one was getting away with anything. Out it all came. Every incompatibility it is possible to imagine was rolled out, displayed to the public, named and numbered, analysed and re-analysed... and before you could say "heavy" it was all over. Pity, really - I could have lived with those incompatibilities for quite a bit longer. It's amazing how compatible I can find myself with a guy with a wonderful smile and a great body... Oh, yes, be careful how you judge me, folks, I'm not as deep as I may seem. Hidden shallows, I've got, me, if you get my meaning. *(He pauses.)* It's the words - the words ruin everything, every time. Which is why being with Jeff is so difficult. Don't get me wrong, he's lovely, but, well, he is a bit obsessed with "the words." Still, this isn't the first time. The first time I had an inkling that he might just be a bit word-fixated was the first time we met - well, the morning after the first time we met. *(MARK picks up the manuscript and gives it to JEFF. During the following, JEFF puts the papers down in his area and sits as if using the computer. MARK puts down the remote control.)* We'd had a good night - no problems in that department at any stage of our relationship, I'm glad to say - but he wasn't in bed when I woke up. *(He starts to unbutton his shirt.)* A bit of a disappointment. *(He undoes another button.)* Don't get excited, this is as far as it goes on the nudity front. *(MARK walks into JEFF's area, the lights changing as he arrives. MARK does his shirt back up again during the following.)* Hallo.

JEFF: Oh, hi. Sleep well?

MARK: Yes, thanks. You didn't?

JEFF: I woke up with a really good idea so I had to rush out here and write it down.

MARK: I woke up with a really good idea, too, but never mind...

JEFF: You mean...

MARK: Yes, I do. Still... *(They both smile. JEFF turns back to the computer.)* I'd better go now. I'm working today.

JEFF: Oh, fine.

MARK: I'd like to see you again, if that's...

JEFF: I don't want anything heavy. Sorry.

MARK: I'm sorry, too. You see, I have this peculiar affliction. I set myself up to say something like "I'd like to see you again" which means, um, well, I'd like to see you again, but d'you know what happens? What happens is, I set myself up to say that, but what I actually say is "I want you to marry me, live with me, never spend a minute of your time in the company of anyone but me and die in my arms at the age of ninety-seven." No wonder you felt threatened. Sorry.

JEFF: OK, I take your point. It's just...

MARK: *(to the audience)* Watch out for that one, too. I always distrust sentences that begin "It's just... ." Because it rarely is.

JEFF: The last guy I went out with was, I thought, exactly what I wanted. The looks, the interests, the tastes, the imagination, the empathy, etc., etc., etc.. And he really hurt me, because he made me feel very loved and very secure but he was lying all the time. He said all the right words at all the right moments. At the beginning, just as you did, he said "I'd like to see you again," then, a bit later, "I really like you," then "I love being with you, you make me feel so relaxed,"then "I hope you don't mind me saying this, but I've fallen in love with you." I was ecstatic when he said things like that. I didn't have to guess at his feelings, I didn't have to read between the lines of everything he said - he just told me, openly, and, I thought, honestly, in words. But he never meant any of it. Any of it. When we finally split up - and he dumped me, it wasn't the other way round - he told me all about the other guys he'd been seeing and he didn't care at all that I was hurt. I said, sounding uncannily like a housewife in a 1950's weepie, "But you said you loved me..." and a really horrible smile came over his face. *(He pauses.)* So, I'm a bit sort of tender at the moment.

MARK: You mean, you're suspicious of the words now?

JEFF: God, no, I need the words. Otherwise how do I know where I stand with a guy? It's just the guys I'm suspicious of, now.

MARK: I see. I understand. Sort of. It won't stop you seeing me again, though, will it? Just platonically, if you like.

JEFF: I don't know.

(There is a long awkward pause.)

MARK: What are you writing?

JEFF: A play. I don't regard my job in the box office as a career for life, you'll be surprised to hear. This is where my heart lies.

MARK: I see. Even though working in a box office introduces you to fab sexy guys like me?

JEFF: Well, yes... but that doesn't happen every day.

MARK: What's it about? Your play.

JEFF: Not much, at the moment. In my head it's a hard-hitting social issues drama about the plight of the homeless, but on paper - on paper it's a mess. The trouble is, you see, I'm trying to create characters who are inarticulate, who haven't the language, the vocabulary, to counter the clever doubletalk of the politicians and social workers they are faced with, but I can't do it. I can't write people who find it difficult to express themselves. *(He pauses.)* I saw this documentary on TV a while back. It was about street violence. This woman, in her late thirties, Northern, was asked how she felt about her son beating another lad up so badly that he'd not fully recovered two years later. Any number of emotions were written across her face - guilt, defensive anger, confusion, embarrassment, you name it - and she struggled for what seemed like ages, before saying: "I can't find the words." That was it. She just didn't have the vocabulary to express her feelings verbally. But if that hadn't been a documentary, if that had been a play, she'd have had to have the vocabulary. No writer, with the odd exception, could resist the urge to give the woman a big speech at such an emotional moment, even though the only words she could use - guilt, anger, confusion, embarrassment - would sound like empty clichés, hollow and unreal, not one of them coming close to expressing what the looks crossing her face were saying. Her feelings, you see, were expressed better because she couldn't fix words to them. The words would have been a clue, yes, but the face told the whole story. It's this truth in inarticulacy that I want to capture, but I can't.

MARK: Have you tried?

JEFF: Oh, yes, I've tried. Last week I went through the whole of Scene 1, taking out anything that seemed too clever, self-knowing or literary, and trying to fashion the little that was left into something that still told the story clearly and indicated what everyone was thinking and feeling. I tried, I suppose, to write just what was visible at the tip of the iceberg rather than describing everything that was going on under the water. But it was a disaster; I thought, "The actors won't know what they're supposed to be doing from one minute to the next." So I tried to indicate the facial expressions and body language they'd be using so that, like the woman in the documentary, they'd be able to express themselves without words, and I thought I was doing quite well until I tried to act out what I'd written in front of the mirror. I just looked constipated. So I had to put some words in - I had to. It would appear that I can't write characters who just act on their feelings, leaving it up to us, on the outside, to work out what those feelings must be: I always have to have them filling the gaps with words, explaining how they feel. I'm too articulate myself, that's the trouble.

MARK: Oh you poor thing.

JEFF: Yes, that did sound a bit fey, didn't it? But you see what I mean, don't you?

MARK: I think I do.

JEFF: There's another thing worrying me, too. Who am I, with my middle-class, educated background, to be trying to create working-class characters who can't express themselves? Isn't that just the most patronizing thing possible? Isn't it?

MARK: I don't know. So many middle-class writers just write about middle-class people that it's good you're having a go at putting someone else on the map, I guess.

JEFF: So you think I should persevere?

MARK: Why not? It's all good experience.

JEFF: That's true. *(He smiles.)* Thanks.

MARK: *(to the audience)* I should have known then there'd be trouble. His last boyfriend used all the right words and he lapped them up gladly, only to be let down - but he still says he needs to hear them. And he can't write the way he wants to write because he's impelled to use words when he knows silence and body language would be better. Is it just me, or do you think he sounds pathological? *(He pauses. To JEFF.)* I'm late for work.

JEFF: I'm sorry. There I am, gabbing away.

MARK: Never mind. *(There is a pause.)* Shall we swap phone numbers, then?

JEFF: Well, um... let me write yours down.

MARK: You don't want to give me your number?

JEFF: Well...

MARK: You do want to see me again?

JEFF: Oh, yes, definitely. It's just...

MARK: *(to the audience)* Uh-oh...

JEFF: It's just I'm naturally pessimistic, you see.

MARK: Right.

JEFF: Well, a lot of people take your number and then never call...

MARK: I get it. You don't want to give me your number because you'll feel rejected if I don't call you?

JEFF: Yes, that's it.

MARK: But if I don't have your number I can't call you anyway.

JEFF: That's true, but at least I'd know you weren't calling me because you couldn't call me, not because you didn't want to.

MARK: If I felt the same, if I didn't give you my number because I'm scared of rejection - which I am, as it happens, but I'm learning to live with it - then we'd be guaranteed never to meet up again. That's ridiculous.

JEFF: You could come to the theatre again.

MARK: That's true, I could, but it seems a bit too much like begging to me. Why can't we both put our necks on the line, both make ourselves a bit vulnerable?

JEFF: I hate rejection.

MARK: So do I. But I'm prepared to trust you.

JEFF: OK. Yes, actually, you're right. You can have my number too.

MARK: Good.

JEFF: You will call me, won't you?

MARK: Unless you call me first. *(MARK moves out of JEFF's area during the following; the lights change as he enters his own area. To the audience)* Generally speaking, the guys you want to see again don't call you; the creeps you spent the night with in a drunken stupor call you incessantly until you threaten to tell their wives. But, just for once, I was in luck. Jeff called me. We met up, we met up again... and, yes, we had fun. *(He switches on the fan and sits in front of it.)* Three weeks later, he told me he loved me. I said, "I'm really pleased," and I was, but I didn't say I loved him. He was disappointed, I could tell, but, well, I wasn't going to lie to him. I strongly suspected then that, in a while, I could love him, but I didn't love him then, so I didn't say it. A week later he said:

JEFF: *(entering MARK's area)* I spoke to Brian yesterday - my old school friend, you remember? - and he said "You keep on mentioning this Mark. Who is he?" And I didn't know.

MARK: I'm sorry? You didn't know? What does that mean?

JEFF: Well, I was about to say "He's my new man" when it occurred to me that calling you "my man" would make you sound like a commodity, a possession, and you're not - nor would you want to be. And it made me realize that I have no idea what we are.

MARK: I see.

JEFF: For example, we're not a "couple" are we? We don't wear matching loafers, finish each other's... um...

MARK: Sentences? Oh, ha-dee-ha!

JEFF: - and we don't spend our Sundays walking round Habitat arguing. Yet.

MARK: So we're "partners"?

JEFF: Well, we don't run a small business together, do we? No, sounds too quasi-legal to me.

MARK: "Boyfriends"?

JEFF: No. No. Sorry. I have a real problem with the word "boyfriend". If you're my "boyfriend" I have to be fifteen, wear lots of pink, have my hair in bunches, metalwork more intricate than the Forth Bridge on my teeth and answer to the name of Tiffany.

MARK: You've just described my ex, Stuart, more or less.

JEFF: Apart from the name.

MARK: And the age. Wrong side of forty, that one, I discovered. Facelift. Tummy tuck.

JEFF: Really?

MARK: Really. OK, so "boyfriend" is out. "Lovers"?

JEFF: Problems there, too. If I think of a "lover" I find myself magically transported back to the 1970s. Flares. Chest wigs. Sideburns. I find myself in a kitchen in the 1970s...

MARK: Macramé pot holders. Lots of beige. Pet rocks.

JEFF: - and in this kitchen is a suburban housewife, up to her Marigold tops in washing-up suds, gazing out of the window and dreaming - dreaming of a man in black from top to toe, his trousers skin-tight to the knee, his hair bouffant but controlled, his Zapata moustache giving him that air of exotic mystery she first experienced in Ibiza...

MARK: He doesn't sound bad, actually...

JEFF: Oh, please. It's an awful image. But that's what I see when you say "lover". That's the trouble. Also, to me, the word "lover" doesn't seem to have any emotion attached to it. It seems to be all about sex. It says "person who makes love" rather than "person who loves."

MARK: So. We're not a couple, partners, boyfriends or lovers - what are we then?

JEFF: Well, that's just what I'm asking you.

MARK: Does it matter? If we happen to hit on the right word, will it make anything better?

JEFF: Well, it would make it easier to explain.

MARK: Explain? Does it really need explanation? We have a relationship, that's all anyone needs to know, if they need to know anything.

JEFF: They'd need to know what sort of relationship, wouldn't they?

MARK: Why? Why not just let them guess? If they can be bothered, that is;

after all, no-one's even a hundredth as interested in our relationship as we are.

JEFF: Brian's very interested.

MARK: Brian needs to get himself a life, by the sound of it.

JEFF: Also, to be honest, it would help me. I don't know how to think about this - about us - I've got no terms of reference.

MARK: You've raised insecurity to an art form, Jeff, you really have. It doesn't matter at all what we are, what title we give whatever it is we've got. With the exception of the times when we have conversations like this, I am always extremely comfortable in your company, and that's all that matters to me.

JEFF: Thank you. That's a definition of sorts.

MARK: It wasn't meant as one.

JEFF: I'm sorry, I've offended you. It's just... *(MARK looks at the audience as if to say "Here we go again.")* It's just that I feel better if I can say to myself "Mark wants to be known as my... whatever", so that I don't misrepresent you, either to other people or to myself. The word "relationship" is so tricky; it stretches from the casual to the committed and always requires qualification. That's why I'm pleased you said you feel comfortable with me...

MARK: Most of the time.

JEFF: - most of the time, because, when Brian asks me about you again, I can say "We're very comfortable together" and it'll give him more of an idea of how we are. Just as it's helped me.

MARK: God, you are desperate, aren't you? Any crumb of comfort you can pick up, you scrabble madly for it.

JEFF: Yes, you're right. I can't bear uncertainty - it really frightens me. I need to hear things in black and white - if you know what I mean! - then I feel more secure. Hearing the words always makes me more secure.

MARK: Even if they're lies?

JEFF: I didn't know he was lying to me, and his words made me feel good. At the time.

MARK: You're a sad case, you really are.

JEFF: Sorry.

MARK: Don't be. You're sweet as well.

JEFF: Oh, thanks.

MARK: And if I find out you've told Brian I said that, you're dead.

JEFF: Fine.

(There is a pause.)

MARK: Lots of people can live quite comfortably with uncertainty, you know; my parents, for example. They lived with the suspicion that I was gay for years, ever since my Mum found me miming to a Doris Day record with a tea-cosy on my head at the age of seven, but they never said anything, never tried to get a definite statement from me, one way or the other. I thought they knew; all the time I was in the closet I assumed it was bloody obvious that I was a raging queen and was hideously self-conscious about all my mannerisms, clothes, choice of music etc. etc. So when I finally came out and they said they'd often wondered but had never assumed, never felt they *knew* in the way that other people claimed they did, I was amazed. *(He pauses.)* I've never told you this, have I? My coming-out drama. I was twenty-eight. Two days before Christmas, it was; Christmas Eve Eve as my family jokily calls it. I'd decided a week before that the moment I arrived at my folk's place I'd tell them all - Mum, Dad, both my brothers and my sister-in-law. So I get home. No brothers, no sister-in-law; they haven't got there yet. Mum's in the kitchen, Dad's pottering around in his study. Having been mortified with terror all week, I'm hopping about like an incontinent by a waterfall, trying desperately to look normal and relaxed. I go into my Dad's study. *(A strangled falsetto.)* "How are you, Dad?" *(He coughs. Normal voice.)* "Sorry. How are you, Dad?" A couple of minutes of agonizingly banal conversation. I don't dare talk to my Mum. I pick up *The Independent.* Huge headline at the top of page two - a semi-comic article - "Don't forget: a homosexual isn't only for Christmas." God - how did they know? Who the hell told *The Independent* about me? So bang goes my cool reading - the - paper routine. I'm about to explode when Mum asks me to cut the bread for lunch. And it's too much for me. Two minutes later I say "Mum, I'm gay" and burst into tears. Like you do. She hugs me, she cries, Dad comes in and I tell him, and he just says "You're my son, what's the problem?"... and I've done it. I've actually done it. So there I am, loaf of Budgen's wholemeal in one hand, breadknife in the other, tears pouring down my face, shaking with relief having gone through the most important and terrifying moment of my life, and Mum says "Look, this is all very well, but we've still got to get lunch ready." Got no sense of occasion, my mother. And the others were the same. I told them an hour or so later, once they'd got settled in and had their lunch. David was so concerned he nearly put the newspaper down. And Ed showed his acceptance by being the first person to make a joke about it. My family has this little tradition: one person is nominated as "Father Christmas" and he or she has to take the presents from under the tree and distribute them to everyone else. So Ed and I are looking idly at the tree and I say, equally idly, "I wonder who'll be Father Christmas this year?" and he says, quick as a flash, "Well, it won't be you, you're the Christmas Fairy." *(He pauses.)* So, that was it. My coming out. I got centre stage for once and what happened - next to nothing. No scenes, no rejections, nothing worthy of soap opera. Over ten years of self-repression released in an hour, and so easily it was almost disappointing. What interested me most, though, was that none of them had *assumed* I was gay - they'd all been waiting for me to say the word, for then they would *know*. No amount of camp gesturing, unsuitable clothing or Abba could tell them differently - the word "gay" could.

JEFF: Words speaking louder than actions.

MARK: For once, yes.

JEFF: You lucky thing, having it so easy.

MARK: It's only in retrospect that it was easy. At the time, and building up to it, it was terrifying. I knew for certain I was gay when I was fourteen, when Mr. Gray the PE teacher made me breathless with lust every time he pounded past in his scarlet satin-effect shorts. But I didn't tell anyone, anyone at all, until I was twenty-eight. And why? Because I was frightened that my parents would reject me. I used a false name when I went out on the scene, just in case someone - can you believe this paranoia - just in case someone found out who I really was and told my parents. As if it would occur to anyone to do that! I lived a double life - Mark by day, Tom by night...

JEFF: Tom?

MARK: Don't ask me why. The crunch came when I met a guy I wanted to try to have a relationship with. I'd met others before, but this one was special. I liked this guy so much I couldn't face having to run away from him, or having a secret, anonymous, dishonest affair with him. I thought to myself, "The only way to solve this is to come out. Then I can have - or at least try to have - the sort of relationship I want: open, honest and comfortable." And I knew that I had to tell my family first. The terror truly set in when I realized that I wouldn't be ready to come out until I knew that I could be rejected and still be strong. When I finally did it, I was fully prepared; there was a chicken in the freezer and a Christmas pudding in the cupboard just in case I had to escape back here. Luckily, of course, I didn't need to, as I was accepted and affirmed on the spot.

JEFF: God, that took some guts.

MARK: Yes, it did.

JEFF: I still can't face it, telling my parents. They're so unyielding, so conventional, and they have such high and - worse than that - specific expectations of me. I know I should come out to them, but the thought terrifies me.

MARK: Well, wait until you're ready, then.

JEFF: I'm not sure when that'll be. You know, I wonder if I'll ever be ready.

MARK: So don't do it.

JEFF: I can't believe you're taking that attitude. Brian says to me, every time I speak to him, "Tell them now. It's the best thing." And I know he's right, but...

MARK: Right for who? Him? He's got no right to make pronouncements like that! No two cases are the same. I was lucky; my parents surprised me by being fine about it. I'm well aware, though, that my experience wasn't typical. It would be ludicrous of me to use myself as an example and say to you: "Oh, it's easy. Get on with it." Because it might not be easy for you - who knows? So, don't let anyone intimidate you into it, and don't force *yourself* into it, either; you should do it because it feels right, not because of any self-imposed sense of obligation.

JEFF: Mark, what would I do without you?

MARK: You'd laugh more, probably. *(The lights fade almost to Black-out. JEFF moves into his area and picks up the manuscript. MARK switches the fan off. The lights come up again on MARK's area. To the audience)* That was six months ago. And, unbelievably enough, we're still together. *(He picks up the CD remote control.)* And this is where you came in...

(He points the remote off stage and presses the on button. Tallis's Spem in Alium begins to play. After a few seconds of music, JEFF comes in with the manuscript.)

JEFF: I've finished it.

MARK: What?

JEFF: I've finished my play. My celebration of inarticulacy.

MARK: Well done.

JEFF: I'd like you to read it. It's a dismal failure, but I'd like you to read it.

MARK: OK.

(JEFF puts the script on the low stool. Then he stands, listening. There is a pause as the music plays on.)

JEFF: What's this? It's gorgeous.

MARK: *Spem in Alium.* The forty part motet by Thomas Tallis.

JEFF: It's... what's that, then, when it's at home? A forty part motet.

MARK: Eight choirs of five voices each, and every single voice singing something different. Forty soloists simultaneously. And it's like a miracle.

JEFF: What's it about?

MARK: *Spem in alium nunquam habui praeter in te, deus Israel...* "I never had hope in any but in you, God of Israel." But for me, the words aren't important. It's the sound that matters. All those words criss-crossing, overlapping, weaving together but remaining totally separate. It's almost like a conversation, but everyone's able to talk and listen at the same time. After a while - listen - *(There is a pause. They listen.)* - after a while, rhythms develop, it pulses. I reckon heaven would sound like this; peaceful but alive, moving forward yet standing still, an exact balance of opposites.

JEFF: Heaven? I didn't think you were religious.

MARK: No, I'm not, but you have to admit there's something in this music that goes beyond the here and now. There's something - dare I say - spiritual about it. In the truest sense.

(There is a pause.)

JEFF: I love you.

MARK: Thank you. I know.

JEFF: How? How do you *know*?

MARK: Well, you've told me several times, but even if you hadn't, I'd know.

JEFF: And you? Do you love me?

MARK: You know exactly how I feel about you.

JEFF: Do I?

MARK: Yes, you do.

(He switches off the music. There is a pause.)

JEFF: Look, we really need to talk.

MARK: I knew that was coming. Well, we're talking. We're always talking.

JEFF: You've never told me you love me.

MARK: I don't need to tell you how I feel. You *know*.

JEFF: Ages ago, you told me your parents had wondered if you were gay, but didn't feel that they knew until you used the word...

MARK: And you feel like that, do you? You 'wonder' whether I love you but the only way you'll 'know' is if I say so?

JEFF: Well, sort of...

MARK: The two statements are completely different. "I'm gay" is a definitive statement which really requires no answer; "I love you", said the way you say it, requires an instant reciprocal response. It's a form of extortion. A says "I love you" to B, and B is trapped. B might quite honestly love A, but if B says "I love you too", then A, who's the paranoid sort, could quite easily believe that B doesn't love A and only said he did because he felt he ought to. But if B - poor old B - doesn't say anything because he'd rather say nothing than say something just because he feels he ought to, then A will get all huffy and think B doesn't love him. So B can never win.

JEFF: So we should never say it. Never say "I love you"?

MARK: Oh, for God's sake, no. Say it whenever you want, but don't say it in order to receive a response. Say it for pleasure of knowing you've said it. Say it for the pleasure you're giving to the person you're saying it to. Just don't hang around panting like a hungry puppy waiting for an answer.

JEFF: You're losing me here.

MARK: I'm losing myself, too. As with everything in life, it's a mass of contradictions.

JEFF: I'm sorry. I know you don't enjoy conversations like this, and I'm forever starting them. I can't help it. I just need a lot of reassurance, I suppose.

MARK: You do. And I really don't mind.

JEFF: Good. You know, I really envy you so much. You're so self-contained and sure of your own value, you don't need to have it reflected back at you at all. How do you manage that? If I can't see any evidence of people valuing me, I can't value myself - it's as if I'm constantly looking in the mirror, needing it to say, "Yes, you are the fairest of them all."

MARK: Well, this mirror's been reflecting back at you for the last seven months, without a break. Only this isn't a magic mirror that can speak, it's a real one. It may show you the warts, the paranoias, the foibles, the irritating personality traits, all the things you really don't want to see, but let me tell you what its principal virtue is: it's still here. And it plans to stay here.

JEFF: Does that mean that...?

MARK: Don't try and trap me into saying anything more.

JEFF: Why don't you ever say how you really feel?

MARK: Because, I suppose, like the woman in the documentary, "I don't have the words." The main difference between her and me is, of course, that she was genuinely inarticulate, whereas I do have the vocabulary to express myself but deliberately choose not to, and I'll tell you why: I hate being misinterpreted. Say something definitive and a paranoid or a cynic will disbelieve it; say something vague, and a romantic or an obsessive will find within it a kernel of profound truth which he'll follow to the ends of the earth. And when it come to relationships, to love, call it what you will, I'm not prepared to be compromised.

JEFF: I see. You've thought about this a lot haven't you?

MARK: Well, I've had to. I knew one day I'd have to justify myself to you.

JEFF: Ouch. You make me sound like an ogre.

MARK: Well, in your own quiet way, you are. You take hold of things and you never let go. You worry away at them, tearing at them with your sharp little teeth until they're in complete tatters, and then you look down at them, torn and bleeding at your feet, and... and you apologize. And ask them if they love you.

JEFF: I'm...

MARK: You were going to say you were sorry then, weren't you? Well, don't. It's part of you. A dalmatian might as well apologize for being spotty. *(He pauses.)* Look, I'm sorry, too, in a way. You need me to say that I love you, don't you? It's almost pathological in you. Well, I acknowledge that need, I completely understand it, but I can't change. I'm here. I've been here - with you - for seven months. I've never hit you. I've never not phoned when I've said I'd phone. I've never been unfaithful. I've never criticized your dress sense...

JEFF: Why do you mention that?

MARK: Aha! Paranoia again!

JEFF: It's the white jeans, isn't it? You never really approved of those, did you?

MARK: I never said so, did I? See, you can pick up on unspoken messages when you want to, can't you? Or can you only pick them up when they're negative and you don't really want them confirmed in words? Is that it? Don't answer that. Back to the plot. You see what I'm getting at, don't you? I'm here. I've been here. I'm staying here.

JEFF: I do see it. I know exactly what you're saying.

MARK: But you still want a definitive statement?

(There is a long pause.)

JEFF: Yes. Please.

MARK: It would be so easy just to say what you want me to say. So easy. But I can't.

JEFF: Oh, Mark...

MARK: I'm sorry. Like you, I've been hurt. Hurt very badly. Hurt by someone who said all the right things at all the right times, but didn't mean them - just like your ex. So I've been there, you see. Been there, done that, worn the T-shirt, cried the tears, kicked the teddy bear...

JEFF: You kicked your teddy bear!

MARK: No way! It was *his* teddy bear. Stuffing everywhere. Best parting gesture I ever made.

JEFF: I'm beginning to understand, now. This whole thing, this whole conscious-inarticulacy thing, it isn't just an intellectual pose, there's emotion behind it. You're frightened. Someone hurt you by using words and not meaning them, by promising things he wasn't prepared to give, and as a result you've locked yourself into a padded cell. You've condemned yourself to never being spontaneous, always self-consciously editing everything you say before you say it so that you won't let something slip that could render you just that little bit vulnerable. You forget that not everyone's like our exes - not every man who says "I love you" is lying. Me, for instance. I have, I admit, said it several times, and every time I've said it I've been hurt by your response but I've never regretted saying it, not once. I've made myself vulnerable, I've got myself hurt - and yet I haven't left you, have I? I've been here. Despite the uncertainty, the pain, I've been here. And you know why.

MARK: Of course I do.

JEFF: Mark, you've got to unlock that cell and set yourself free.

MARK: Oh, please! Where are we, California? I'm sorry, I don't buy into all this "speak your feelings" stuff, not when the only words we can use to express ourselves are the sad old clichés of literature or psychology. We need a new language, one that can't be misinterpreted or misused, one that isn't obscured by centuries of cultural redefinition. When that language arrives, I'll use it; until then I'll keep silent. And have the satisfaction of knowing that I'll never be misinterpreted.

JEFF: Well, of course you won't be, if you never say anything.

MARK: But I do say things. I don't have to speak, to use words, to communicate, do I? *(He pauses.)* OK, here goes. You want to hear it, so I'll say it...

JEFF: Oh, God. Don't do this to me. Don't say it just to make me happy, say it because you want to.

MARK: I want to. *(MARK slowly approaches JEFF and gives him a warm hug. Then, still holding JEFF, he kisses him lightly on his lips.)* There.

JEFF: That's it?

MARK: That's it.

JEFF: Well, that'll do.

MARK: It'll have to.

(There is a pause. JEFF finally smiles. He kisses MARK. Without any bidding, Spem in Alium begins to play again from where it left off. The fan comes on and the pages of JEFF's script blow across the stage. The kiss becomes more passionate, the hug more intense. The music swells, the papers swirl... Slow fade to Black-out.)

END

Manny's Party

by
Geoff Saunders

First performed as a rehearsed reading at the Goodrich Theatre, Putney, on 23rd March 1997. Subsequently performed in a full production at the Actors Centre, London, on 11th August 1997, with the following cast:

Cassandra .... *CJ Lampard*

Directed by Geoff Saunders

With thanks to Caroline Ferris

Characters

Cassandra

Darkness. A spotlight comes up. CASSANDRA walks into the light clutching a glass of gin and tonic. She wears an expensive dress, is beautifully made up and is ever so slightly drunk.

CASSANDRA: Two minutes to go. It's all set: finger buffet for thirty-five on the big table in the conservatory, lots of champagne chilling nicely in every bucket we could lay hands on and ice from every freezer in the street, bless them all... nice dress, earrings, hair, nails, lipstick, blusher, shoes - oh, God, mayonnaise on left toe, crisis crisis - yes, it's all there, all set. And in two minutes it officially begins. They'll all come pouring in, all of Manny's colleagues from work, all in their beautiful suits and gorgeous shoes and all with gleaming hair and gleaming teeth and all the women with row upon row of gleaming little pearls.

And I hate the lot of them. And I hate these parties.

Manny says, "Oh, darling, isn't it time you had one of your little parties?" and I snap to attention and consult my little book and the whole process rolls into action. Note how it's *my* little party; he makes it sound like a treat, a gift from him to me. Well, it's *his* friends that get invited, he can't bear mine - "They're all bloody housewives," he says, "nothing to talk about but baby poo and gardening" - and, guess what, I have to do all the bloody work. So it's no treat. And, guess what, I'm on my third gin already.

I'm going to wait for Clive Thingy - Arrowsmith - his boss, great oily whale of a man, his suit stretched over him like the lagging on the immersion heater, but less attractive... I'm going to wait for him and give him a warm and friendly handshake, a warm and friendly kiss perhaps, and wipe this bloody mayonnaise on his trouser leg. Childish but fun.

Doorbell doorbell. Charm, Cassandra, charm.

(Sheflings open the door, which we can't see. Neither can we see any of the people who come through it. To them.) Rhona! Kelvin! Do come in!

(To us.) Bloody Rhona Starkey from the typing pool. Manny's favourite brainless bimbo of the moment. A dress so small she needs a search party to find it, breasts so large and preposterously underwired you could lose Sherpa Tensing in her cleavage for decades and, God, she's drunk already!

(To RHONA.) What's that, Rhona? Oh, yes, it's bonza to see you too, dear. Yes, it will be a ripper of a party, I'm sure.

(To us.) Australian.

(To RHONA.) Oh, of course, dear. Up the stairs, second on the left, don't fall over the baby seat!

(To us.) Though in her state it might help her to use it. Might save the pedestal mat from harm, too...

(To KELVIN.) Are you going to wear your jacket, Kelvin, or shall I hang it up for you?... Oh, fine, yes, on the floor, anywhere, don't mind me... The... er... booze is just through there, dear... No, it's only champagne. Sorry... You've brought your own cans? Good idea. Good idea... Yes, through there.

(To us.) Mail room. Earring. Tattoo.

Doorbell doorbell. Where's Manny? I know this is meant to be my bloody party but he could come and open the door to his awful colleagues.

(To MANNY, calling.) Manny, Manny dear, could you...? ... Oh, no matter, I'm sure that's more important... No, dear, no, no irony intended. Will you come out and see a few people in a minute? When the snooker's finished?... Thank you, dear.

Doorbell doorbell.

(She flings open the door. To ALISON.) Alison, dear! Come in! Lovely to see you. *(She insincerely "air kisses" ALISON with plenty of "mwah" sounds.)* Yes, fine and you?... Super. Lovely dress.

(To us) Bright green. She looks like a stick of bloody celery.

(To ALISON.) Yes, of course, dear, up the stairs, second on the left, don't fall over the baby seat!

(She closes the door. To MANNY.) Manny!... Yes, I'm glad Steve Davis is doing well, too.

(To us.) Remind me, next time I see Steve Davis I'm going to march right up to him and punch him up the throat.

I could hide. I could run upstairs and open the big wardrobe in the back room and hide. They'd never think to look for me in there. God, why does it have to be me that opens the door and does all the smiling? Manny should be here, or he should be in the conservatory tackling the champagne. Apart from anything, it's undignified, the poor hostess standing by the door like a lackey while the guests rampage about the house without so much as a by-your-bloody-leave.

(To KELVIN.) Yes, of course, Kelvin, dear, up the stairs, second on the left, don't fall over the baby seat!

(To us.) I can smell cigarette smoke. Oh, God! Manny will throw a fit!

(To ALISON.) Oh, Alison, darling, hello. Manny's hoping to be around soon, he's dealing with some important business just now... Oh yes, he often works at home... Yes, he does. I wish he'd come out, actually, as I'm sure you'd like a drink and I can't really leave the door... Oh, is that one of Kelvin's cans? I can't see you as a bitter drinker, really. Well, well.

(To us.) Yorkshire.

(To KELVIN.) Back so soon, Kelvin?... Oh, I see, locked herself in, has she? Does she often... Oh, I see. It's funny how often people have rows on the way to parties. I often think throwing a party is like setting up a group therapy session... No, dear, that was just a little joke. Wait till Manny appears, he can tell you all about therapy, the poor dear.

(To ALISON.) Alison, it's just crossed my mind - if Rhona Starkey is

locked in the loo up there, then where did you...? Oh, you used the other one. Oh good.

(To us.) Oh no! There's a definite suspicion of a smirk playing around her two-shades-of-lip-liner, gloss-and-frosted-seal lips, and I know why. She's smirking at my *en suite* facilities, I can tell. "Update, Manny," I've said more than once, but, oh, no, it's "retro chic" - i.e. cheapo trendy - to have an avocado suite and a bead curtain and a bloody pet rock in the bloody corner, he says, but of course it's my taste that's under the microscope as far as she's concerned, and she's smirking.

(To MANNY.) Manny! Do come out and say some hellos, won't you?

Doorbell doorbell.

(To KELVIN.) Kelvin, there's one in the outhouse, just through there. Fight your way past the spin dryer and the lawn mower and it's all yours. *(She opens the door.)* Clive!

(To us.) Only Clive Arrowsmith would come to a party here, in this Crescent, in full view of the neighbours - how could he! - in a track suit! A track suit, I ask you! Over that pudgy, wobbly body. He looks like a giant sock filled with custard. We dress up for his parties, I can tell you, but what do you get from him? We get all the studied insult of can't-be-bothered casual clothing.

(To CLIVE.) Clive, do come in. *(She kisses CLIVE, extending her foot to wipe the mayonnaise on his leg.)*

(To us) Got him!

(To CLIVE.) No, it wasn't a bring-a-bottle party, so it's quite all right. We've got plenty here, don't you worry. Do go through. Monica not with you?

(To us.) That was below the belt, Cassandra. You know for a fact Monica found out last week he was having it off with Sharon Barnacle (or whatever her name is) from Avis Recknall.

(To CLIVE.) Oh, I'm so sorry. Funny time to get hay fever, really, in November. Still, can't be helped. Poor Monica. Do go through!

Doorbell doorbell. Manny!

(She opens the door. A flurry of air kissing follows. To several people.)

Ahmed! Benjy! Samantha! Gerry! Maxine! Sarah!... No, sorry, I really can't get used to the idea of calling you "Sparky"!

(To BARRY.) Barry! Lovely to see you! No Bernard? Oh, dear, a party's not complete without the Barry and Bernard Barbara Streisand Experience... He's left you for a car mechanic? Oh, Barry! Look, find me again later and we'll sit on the stairs and talk about what bastards men are.

(To MANNY, calling.) Manny!

(To BARRY.) No, things are fine, Barry, just fine. Manny's just... in there... watching the bloody snooker.

(To the others.) Go through, go through, all of you. Help yourselves - what was that?

(To BARRY.) Rhona's up there, Barry. Please go up and see what that crash was.

(To ALISON.) More glasses, Alison? They're in the cupboard with... Yes, the cupboard with the wonky shelf and the door that has just come off in your hand...

(To KELVIN.) Oh, Kelvin, there you are. Back to the outhouse with you. Dustpan and brush, please! Chop chop!

(To ALISON.) No, don't worry, they weren't expensive crystal - not *that* expensive, anyway.

(To MANNY.) Yes, Manny, I did hear two crashes. Why don't you come out and...? No, dear, I'm so sorry, of course he's about to pot the green and of course it's important...

Doorbell doorbell. *(She opens the door to several people.)* Barbara! Steve! Ruth! Yes, come in! *(A flurry of air kissing.)* Go through! Go through!

(To RUTH.) Yes, of course, Ruth, up the stairs, second on the left... Oh, of course. Someone's locked in there, thinks it's amusing, I suppose. You'll have to use the *en suite*. Through the master bedroom - first right - keep going until something avocado hoves into view!

(To GERRY.) Gerry, hallo. Aren't you going to...? No, that's fine, I could do with some company. Manny's in there, hard at work, poor poppet, but I'm sure he'll be out soon. How are things in the thrusting world of accounts, Gerry? All going well?... Oh, super, super, sounds great, really

creative and special, but then you've always had great ideas, haven't you? I remember spotting you at that party the week you joined the company - oh, yes, I was there, but of course you didn't notice me - and I remember thinking "He'll go far." And here we are, ten years later, and you have. You're at the top. Of accounts. And you're still looking, if I may say so, as dynamic as ever. So many men start to lose their figures as they get older, but you, you're as slim and taut and - and - as you've always been. I bet there are still hearts fluttering for you in the typing pool... Really? That's a bit of a change of direction for you, isn't it?... Oh, well done, well done, Gerry, that's so brave, so selfless of you. Not everyone would give up a damn good job in Accounts to join the priesthood. I'm impressed... Yes, do go through.

(To us.) Damn him. Sexiest man to come through this door in years and he wants to be a priest. Unless he was just saying that to get away from me. Not that I was planning to drag him upstairs and deflower him in the master bedroom with everyone trotting past to laugh at my avocado *en suite*. But at least I could dream. Can't dream about a priest, though, can I? *(She pauses.)* Then again...

(To RUTH.) Oh, yes, Ruth, it's true, you don't see so much avocado these days, do you? Yes, it's our little *homage* to Seventies chic; so amusing, don't you think?... Do go through... No, I'm fine here on my own. Do go through.

(To us.) We used to have lovely parties when I was a girl. My mother had to do nothing: she got the caterers in. Steadman and Gorse, they were called, two little men with moustaches, helped by a funny woman who unfortunately had a moustache as well. Mr Steadman was the cook, Mr Gorse the organizer, the unnamed woman did everything she was organized to do, and they were brilliant. The dining room would be awash with candles and white starched tablecloths; it was like a Catholic high altar to the God of entertaining. Mr Gorse would become the barman, the woman the waitress, and Mr Steadman would glide about as if he were on castors, appearing at precisely the right moments to open doors, place ashtrays or even - as on one spectacular occasion when Uncle Edward Bertram decided to recreate a Vietnam battle in the morning room - even ejecting elements deemed likely to damage the furniture.

And Mummy would glide, too, through her lovely party, her head slightly on one side as if taking an interest in what people were saying even when no-one was talking to her, holding a wine glass that never seemed quite empty and never seemed quite full, and she'd smile the most angelic smile with absolutely no effort at all. She was wonderful.

When I was tiny, of course, I wasn't supposed to take part. My first official party was just after my fifteenth birthday, when I put my hair up rather extravagantly and wore a terribly adult dress and blushed continuously for three whole hours, standing by the French windows toying with a cocktail stick because I had absolutely no idea of how to get rid of it. In the years before that, I perfected the art of turning up unexpectedly in my night things and winning the hearts of all the adults present. I was such a tart, looking back. I'd get into bed very carefully, so as not to crease my nightie, and spend the next hour or so carefully disarranging my hair so that I'd look appealingly tousled and yet sleek at one and the same time. Then I'd wait for the noise level to rise a bit, which meant they were all getting a bit tiddly and would no doubt look very pink and jolly when I appeared, and I'd descend the stairs very slowly, trying hard to combine looks of infinite tiredness and adult insouciance, rubbing my eyes with my lovely pink fingers - but not too hard - and emitting unhappy but sweet little bleats. I'd wait until the noise level reached some sort of crescendo, then push the dining-room door open and gaze upwards, with doe-like eyes and trembling lips, at whoever happened to be nearest.

Invariably my father, my gorgeous father, his hair slicked back, his chest wide and comforting under his immaculate dinner jacket - those shoulders! - invariably he'd spot me and glide towards me, smiling, and whisk me up with one strong arm and hold me near the light so everyone could see me. And, of course, a hush would fall and I'd blink and let fall a little tear and of course they'd all love me and coo and smile and say "Aah"... I loved it. Belle of the ball, star of the show, and there beside me my favourite man in the whole world with his big black moustache heartbreakingly sprinkled with grey.

I've heard it said that women marry men who remind them of their fathers. Well, I'm not at all convinced. Manny might have been like my father once, but it can't have lasted long, the resemblance, and I certainly can't remember it. He's nothing like my father *now*, anyway... He's mean-minded, cruel, heartless, arrogant, uncaring and he's gone off sex, the bastard. With me, anyway. He's probably done it with Rhona Starkey in some grubby back room at work and convinced her that he loves her. Stupid cow. Still, that's how he got me. Coy chats over the photocopier, touching hands in the lift, then an awful thrash in the filing room next to my office. Stupid, stupid cow. I should have known it wouldn't work when I overheard him telling Andy "Belch the loudest ha ha" Medhurst that he'd "plucked me from the typing pool." I was Marketing Support Manager, for God's sake! Higher up the ladder than he was! But of course the moment we were married I became "Manny's Wife." And "No wife of mine will go out to work." And, stupid stupid stupid cow, I thought: "How lovely! He wants to take care of me." And he has, I suppose.

Oh, Daddy, I do miss you.

(She pauses. To MANNY.) Manny! Manny! Everyone's leaving!... Yes, they are!

(To the others) Party's over! Go home! All of you! No, I'm not feeling well! I'm not feeling well at all, and I haven't felt well for ages!... That's it, Kelvin, pick up your horrible smelly jacket, winkle that sad Antipodean tart out of our bog - yes, bog, Clive, I did say that word, I know all those words, surprisingly enough! - and go! And you, too, Clive, you great lump of blubber in your disgusting, insulting track suit with something or other smeared on the leg! Go! All of you! Go! Go! Go! *(She flings open the door.)* Goodbye! Goodbye! I hope I never see any of you again, ever! And keep off the streets, all of you - If I'm driving past I may just run you over! Goodbye! Goodbye! Goodbye! *(She closes the door.)*

Bog. Bog. Bog.

(To MANNY.) They've all gone, Manny! They've all gone! And they won't be back!

(A long pause.)

And neither will I!

(She looks round the room. Slowly, a smile breaks out on her face.)

Bye, Manny! See you in court!

(And she walks out of the light. END)

Benny's Funeral

by
Geoff Saunders

First performed as a rehearsed reading at the Goodrich Theatre, Putney, on 23rd March 1997, with the following cast:

Morris . . . . *Geoff Saunders*

Directed by Geoff Saunders

Subsequently performed in a full production at the Actors Centre, London, on 11th August 1997, with the following cast:

Morris . . . . *Alan Knight*

Directed by Adrian Brown

Characters
Morris

The lights come up on MORRIS, a cheerful man in his late fifties, sitting in an armchair.

MORRIS: I haven't stopped laughing since Benny died.

I shouldn't have told you that.

It's true though. Three weeks ago last Sunday Benny died and I haven't cried once. Just laughed. I haven't mourned, I suppose. Deirdre, she's been to counselling classes and all that whatnot, she says to me "You should *own* your grief", whatever that means - as if I could give it away. Sometime soon, perhaps, I'll have a good weep and get it all out of my system, but just at the moment there doesn't seem to be anything in my system to start with. There's this big empty space inside me, that's all, and I seem to find everything funny. Don't get me wrong, I miss Benny, I really loved him and I built my whole life round him, and I'm really not sure how I'll go on without him. But I can't stop myself laughing.

Lots of people have said to me "I didn't know Benny had AIDS" and it's really annoyed me. I've spat back, more than once, "He didn't have AIDS. Just because he lived with another man you assume he had AIDS, and you're wrong. It was a heart attack." The idea of a gay man dying of anything other than AIDS amazes people, it doesn't fit in with their idea of gay life. You could get yourself knocked down by a bus and they'd come to your funeral with red ribbons and collecting boxes.

Well, anyway, yes, it was a heart attack. We'd spent hours in the garden - I mow, he weeds, which is a good arrangement because I can't tell a dandelion from an orchid, let me tell you - and we thought we'd treat ourselves to 'Thoroughly Modern Millie' on the video. Now, Benny does the best Carol Channing this side of... of Carol Channing, I suppose, and he was gearing himself up for 'Jazz Baby' and I was getting ready for a good laugh, because it's always funny, no matter how many times I see it, and well, he fell over. "This is new", I thought - I did - "I've never seen him do that before." I really thought that, I'm ashamed to say. Anyway, I laughed, because he did look so funny until I realized what had happened. I went deadly calm, glacial as they say, and I got him comfortable - neither of us saying a word, although he was still alive and his eyes were full of sparkle as usual - and then I phoned the ambulance men, clear and calm and efficient as I could be, and when I got back to him he was dead. I turned off the TV for a moment, but the silence was horrible so I turned it on again. "That wasn't respectful," said Deirdre later, "having Julie Andrews and Mary Tyler Moore and that James Fox prancing about while Benny's lying dead on the floor" but I told her the noise helped me and she made up some psychological stuff to explain my behaviour so I wouldn't feel guilty. I wish she hadn't. It hadn't occurred to me to feel guilty until then. And now I do. Anyway, the ambulance men arrived and they were so good. They had Benny sorted out in a trice, they were ever so nice and gentle with me, and I was so impressed I offered them all coffee and shortbread. They hadn't the time, but they'd have been welcome. One of the ambulance men - pretty boy, lovely lashes - took one look at the TV and said "Oh I'm sorry I'm missing this, it's my favourite film" and I thought "Well, that's given your game away, Butch," and I told him it was on tape and if he wanted to come round sometime, he could borrow it. He never came round, of course.

I shouldn't have told you that.

I didn't laugh then but I've laughed a lot since. For example: the funeral parlour. I'd never in my life visited one, so I was a bit nervous, really, but I thought as it was Benny I'd go along and look at him one last time. And I'm so glad I went on my own, I can tell you. First of all, I'm met at the door by this huge man with a tail coat on and a face as long as next week - the spit of Boris Karloff - and he's got this extremely deep and depressed sort of voice. "Just a moment, Mr. Edwards," he booms, and leads me into a small side room and I'm smiling already. Two women go into the chapel bit and two men with tail coats come out and then the women come out dusting their hands and then I'm ushered in. They have these big mahogany doors and Boris Karloff pushes them open and stands to one side and in I go, feeling dead nervous.

Up at the back, on the floor, there's this crucifix with a Virgin Mary statue - chipped - just dumped on the carpet, not at all artistically arranged and completely missed by the spotlights coming from the ceiling. I suppose they must have a selection of handy artefacts for each religion and bring them out sharpish for each visitor. Anyway, in front of them, and perfectly lit, this time, there's the coffin with Benny in it, and this is when I start to laugh. It's awful, I know, but it's true. You see, Benny could pull the funniest faces; he'd have me in stitches from morning to night when he was in the mood. And what had the laying-out people done? They'd only beggared about with his dentures so he was pulling a face, hadn't they? He looked so daft that I started to snigger. Boris was still hovering in the doorway, so I pulled out my hanky and tried to make sobbing sounds. "I'll leave you with him, sir," he boomed, and I was so relieved. But it got worse. Either side of the religious artefacts were these stereo speakers, one of them with a wicked hiss, and over the speakers was playing a recording of what I can only guess was a Bontempi organ. I almost expected to hear an electronic drumbeat with marimbas and castanets. And what's the tune? It's only 'Abide with me'. Isn't it? *(He mimics the organ.)* Dee... dee dee dee dee... dee dee dee dee dee... I was so pleased when it stopped. There was a moment's silence and I was just beginning to think I could get my face straight enough to leave, when what happened? The tape machine went "Ker-choonk, ker-choonk, ker-choonk" - two three four - *('Abide with Me' once more.)* Dee... dee dee dee dee... And that was too much for me. I had to lean up against the wall, I was laughing that much. I laughed until my eyes streamed, but it wasn't like crying, if you know what I mean. I covered my face with my hanky and made a dash for the door. "You may stay longer if you wish, sir," boomed Boris, but I just sobbed "No, no," and ran for it. The two women I'd seen earlier were outside eating sandwiches - awful smell of fish paste - and as I passed them they jumped up and zoomed inside, one of them saying "I'd lose that Madonna right now, Florence, the next one's Presbyterian."

You know, it's a pity it's not thought tasteful to video a funeral. I wish I'd a tape of Benny's to watch because I can't remember it. Bits before, bits after, but none of the really important middle bit, actually in the crematorium. I can remember arriving. Benny had specifically asked for people to dress cheerfully, and not one of his family wore anything but black. Thinking about it, they're such a miserable lot at the best of times they probably wear black to christenings, weddings, and anniversary celebrations as well - a whole family of the 'Living Dead'. Expensive black it was, too; beautifully cut suits, silk ties, shiny black frocks and hats with veils and, as a co-ordinating feature, all of the ladies had nice black streaks down their faces. Very touching, I'm sure. Lesson one: you can't exude hypocritical emotion with waterproof mascara. God, it made me laugh. I looked at their Freda, the worst of the lot, and I thought "Who invited Chi-Chi the panda to this party?" I could just hear Benny saying "Ooh, what's she come as?" - his favourite line, that one. And every one of the beggars hugged me, which was horrible - being hugged by someone who hates you is the worst, I can tell you. I kept wondering if they were being photographed hugging me - I had the strongest sense of them all watching themselves being nice to me and feeling really compassionate and noble. Bloody hypocrites - some of them hadn't seen Benny for years, ever since they discovered I wasn't just his lodger, but they were all putting on this great show of grief. Their Freda - damn great big black hat like a Pirelli tyre with veiling, trying to look Sophia Loren but coming over all Barbara Cartland - she came wailing up to me: "He was my favourite cousin." And I snapped back, "So that's why you came round to visit so often," knowing full well, as did she, she'd never crossed the threshold of 84 Garrelston

Place in all the fifteen years we'd lived there, and that shut her up. She looked confused, poor cow, and I couldn't resist twisting the knife. "He's not left you anything in his will," I told her. "What little he had will come to me." Which happens to be true.

I was a bit ashamed of myself, really, saying that to Freda - I was also annoyed with her for doing such a convincing job of mourning when all I could do was crack jokes and camp about. The crematorium's all red and cream, you see, like one of those fast food restaurants, and it's not that different atmosphere-wise - you know, overheated, funny smell, full of depressed-looking people - and once I'd pointed that out to Bernard and Cyril we couldn't stop laughing.

Bernard and Cyril - they're a right pair. They'd only turned up in their full leather regalia - chaps, jackets, caps, boots, the lot. "I know Benny wanted colour," Bernard said, "but we couldn't resist it." They got some funny looks, I can tell you. One of Benny's cousins found herself stuck with Cyril at the shindig afterwards and, in a desperate bid to make conversation she asked him, "And what sort of motorbike do you ride?" He put on his campest voice and said, "Oooh, no dear, I've never been on one, they scare me to death." I laughed my head off.

Every time Bernard saw me he'd point at my shirt and say "Nice blouse, Morris", and it made me happy, sort of. You see, I'd got on my sky blue silk, the one Benny really liked. I remember wearing it one day and Benny saying "You're my blue sky, Morris," and I pretended to gag, you know, with my fingers in my mouth. I wish I hadn't. That was one of the few occasions Benny was at all romantic, and I'd gone and spoilt it by being embarrassed and mucking about. Perhaps I didn't spoil it. Perhaps he knew how pleased I was. I'll never know.

It was nice to have friends around me, I can tell you. We had such a laugh - all the same jokes, but with slightly smaller smiles than usual and a sad look in everyone's eyes. And the hugs and kisses from them were real, too, which was good.

Benny's brother Colin came over for a chat, which pleased me. We've always got on well, ever since he discovered we support the same football team. He was so surprised, I can tell you. "Just because I'm an old nance, doesn't mean I can't enjoy a game of soccer," I told him, then gave him one of my twinkly looks. "Anyway, twenty-two beefy fellas in shorts have a certain visual appeal for a man of my leanings," I said, and he roared. We've been friendly ever since. We'd barely started talking at the funeral when that sour-faced wife of his came stomping over to us - deportment has never been her strong point - and started trying to drag him away on some spurious pretext or other. "I'm sorry," he said to me. "You go," I said, "don't get into trouble over me." And he said, "I'll keep in touch, Morris." And he has. He's phoned every other day, just for a few minutes. He sounds just like Benny on the phone, he really does. That ought to hurt, really, but it doesn't. I quite like it. But he has rung - I'm impressed. I can hear her in the background radiating disapproval, but I don't refer to it at all. I bet she'll try to put a stop to it some day. Cow.

Oh, well.

As I say, I hardly remember the service. I remember wanting to cry, as I was convinced that that would prove to Benny's horrible family that I loved him and would miss him, but, no, nothing happened, and I'm sure they thought the worst. I must have said the prayers, sung the hymns, I must have given the little speech I'd written with lots of jokes in, but I didn't cry - I'd have remembered that, surely - and now the whole half-hour is no more than a blur. It's almost as if I read about it in a magazine when I wasn't really paying attention.

A few days ago, Deirdre was round here again, trying to help by putting the crockery away in all the wrong cupboards, and she said to me: "It's a bit like a man losing his wife, this, isn't it?" And I said, "No, dear, it's *exactly* like a man losing his husband." So she said, " Did neither of you feel he had the female role in this relationship?" And I said, "No, dear, neither of us has ever scraped an uneaten dinner into the pedal bin while the other one was out with his mates."

Not that Benny was perfect, let me tell you. He never missed a meal and was kind and attentive and never went off me in the bed department - and I'd always assumed he would, one day, as we got older - but he did play the field a bit, and I didn't like that. He'd pick up other guys on his afternoons off and spend the evening grinning away to himself like he'd just scored a winning goal for England. It made me furious, but I knew I couldn't stop him. He just liked men, different men, men who were a challenge and had to be worked for. I couldn't play hard to get to save my life, not with him, so I suppose it was too easy with me and he had to venture afield for some excitement. Oh, well. There came a point when I actually found myself wishing he had AIDS so he'd have to stay at home and be nursed by me. I had this image of him, dying, and saying "I love only you, Morris, and I should never have gone with anyone else," and me saying, "I forgive you, Benny, because my love is bigger than this." Then I pulled myself up short and gave myself a good talking-to. I'd just wished Benny dying - what a disgusting thought! And I realized, at that moment, that I'd rather have Benny alive and adulterous than dead, and from that moment on I accepted his little weaknesses and peccadilloes and never complained. But what an awful thing to have thought. It makes me ashamed to think of it.

I shouldn't have told you that.

I talked to the priest about that, about wishing Benny dying. The priest - Alan, his name is, he's one of us, looks cute in jeans - Alan said it was quite common to wish our loved ones harm; he said it was the dark side of my love for Benny that had made me feel the way I'd felt, and it wasn't nice but it was quite human and forgivable. Alan's been a great help to me these last weeks, he really has. And he didn't bat an eyelid when I requested that Benny's coffin glide into the flames to the tune of 'Send in the Clowns'. We could have sung it - everyone I know is word-perfect on it. Except Cyril of course - he wouldn't even take to a Sondheim song if that Kylie Minogue sang it. Still, there's no accounting.

I'll like as not cry soon. Something daft will set it off, probably, like an old photo or a film on the telly; or something completely unexpected and more than likely at a really awkward time. I'll tell you, though, if that Dierdre tells me one more time to have a good cry I'll smack her one, because she seems to think it's all I need to feel better and she's wrong. It would help a bit, I know, but it'd take more than a cry to make me feel *really* better. I feel like one of those old sailor dummies in a booth at the seaside. Put in a penny and I fall about laughing. About what, though? Laughing about nothing. That's what I feel like: an empty dummy laughing at nothing. And no amount of crying will solve that, Dierdre, you daft beggar.

I shouldn't have told you all that, should I? Still, you've got to talk to someone.

You've got to. *(END.)*